Tokyo Tower, from the World Trade Center

Credits

Photography by Roger Miller
Design by David Miller
Text by Ron Pilling
Edited by Bonnie Lynn Baer
Writing Coordinated by Sarah Carter
Printed by Dai Nippon Printing Co., Ltd. Tokyo, Japan
Typesetting by Brushwood Graphics, Inc.

Information

Library of Congress Catalog Card Number: 87-080981

ISBN 0-911897-05-4

First Edition 1987

Dedication

David P. Miller

My brother, architect, book designer, business partner, friend, chief critic, and at times my confessor...A book on Tokyo has been our dream since the beginning...I still don't think we look alike...Thanks for being there.

Roger C. Miller

Special Thanks

To everyone in Tokyo who has made this wondrous city what it is today.

A particularly warm thanks to the numerous "momentary friends" who helped a lost and sometimes just confused stranger in his travels.

To the **Japan National Tourist Organization** for their help and assistance in doing this book. Especially to **Mr. Hideo Hamano, Mr. Hideaki Nakazawa, Mr. Naoto Aoyoma,** and **Mrs. Seiko Taniguchi** for their efforts which made this book a much more complete portrait of Tokyo.

To the **Foreign Press Center, Japan** for its continued efforts in assisting writers and photographers working in Japan. A special thanks to **Mr. Shigeyoshi Araki** for his time and efforts on our behalf.

To all the businesses in Japan for their assistance in allowing us to take photographs of their facilities.

To the **Japan Stage Players' Association** for their help and assistance in allowing us to photograph the Kabuki actors. A special thanks to **Mr. Nakamura Shibajaku, VII** for allowing us to take photos of him.

To **Oyakata Tomozuna** for allowing us to take photos of his stable of sumo wrestlers.

To **Mio Kinouchi,** and **Norihisa Katayama** of **The Image Bank, Tokyo** for their assistance and kindness while I was in Tokyo.

To my dedicated mostly hardworking staff without the help of both **Bonnie Lynn Baer** and **Sarah Carter** this book would not exist.

To **Centrabank an NCNB Company** for their efforts and belief in our work and our success. A very special thanks to **H. Lee Boatwright, III, Mike Glump,** and **Gail Houser** for their time and efforts on behalf of the Tokyo book.

Roger C. Miller

Nihombashi Bridge, Imperial Palace

Tokyo Harbor, from Tokyo Tower

CONTENTS

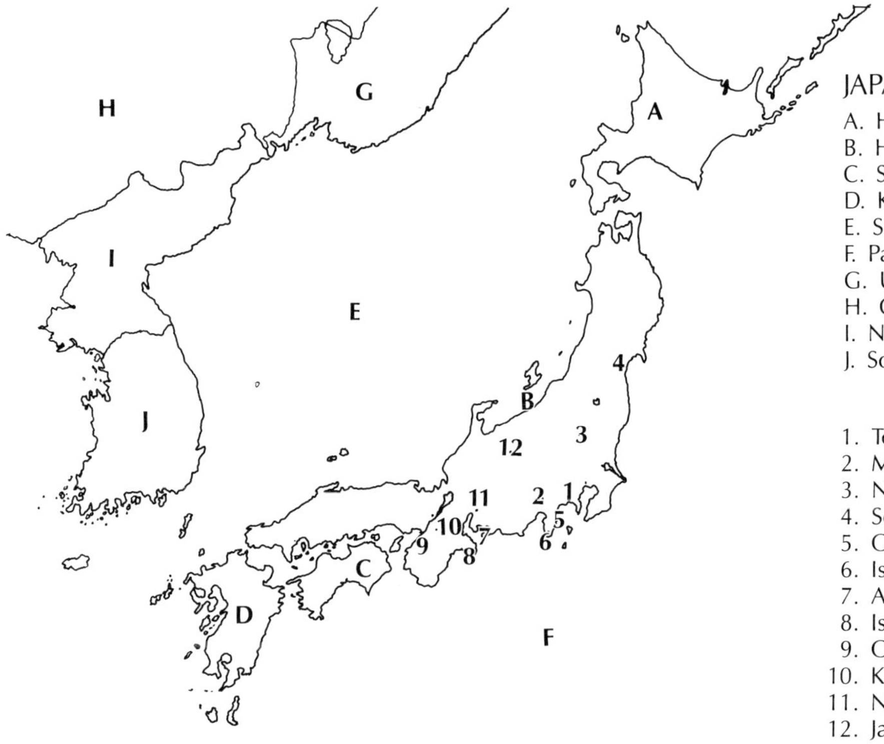

JAPAN
A. Hokkaido
B. Honshu
C. Shikoku
D. Kyusho
E. Sea of Japan
F. Pacific Ocean
G. U.S.S.R.
H. China
I. North Korea
J. South Korea

1. Tokyo
2. Mt. Fuji
3. Nikko
4. Sendai
5. Odwara
6. Isu Hanto Peninsula
7. Atsumi-war Peninsula
8. Ise Peninsula - Toba
9. Osaka
10. Kyoto
11. Nagoya
12. Japan Alps

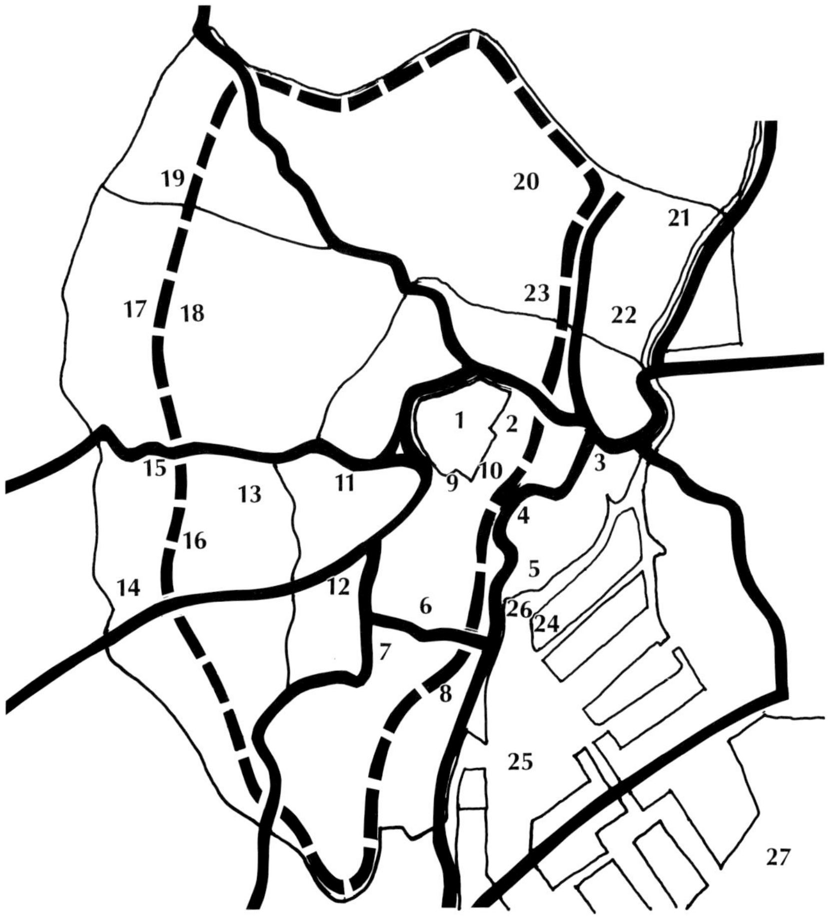

TOKYO
1. Imperial Palace
2. Marunouchi
3. Nihombashi
4. Ginza
5. Tsukiji
6. Shimbashi
7. Shiba
8. Hamamatsucho
9. Kasumigaseki
10. Hibiya
11. Akasaka
12. Roppongi
13. Aoyama
14. Shibuya
15. Meiji Shrine
16. Harajuku
17. Shinjuku West
18. Shinjuku East (Kabukicho)
19. Ikebukuro
20. Ueno
21. Asakusa
22. Asakusabashi
23. Akihabara
24. Toyomi
25. Tokyo Harbor
26. Sumida River
27. Tokyo Bay

Lacquered Temple Guard, Nikko

HISTORY

By 1457, when Ota Dokan, a regional Shogun, built his first castle in what would become Tokyo, Japan had over a thousand years of tradition behind her. It was a feudal nation of warring city-states. The Shogun's stronghold, then called Edo, was an ideal place in war-torn Japan, with the sea at its edge and the mountains nearby.

The village rose to power under Shogun Tokugawa Ieyasu, marking the beginning of a long and prosperous period. Japan was long ruled by minor Shoguns, warrior-statesmen who ruled their city-states pretty much as they pleased. To maintain their power, they kept large armies of samurai, aristocratic, selfless Japanese warriors with unfailing devotion to their leaders. Tokugawa Ieyasu was the first Japanese leader to succeed in subjugating these shoguns, thus forming a national government.

Eventually Edo, as Ieyasu's stronghold, became the most powerful town in the island nation. The official Imperial capital was still in Kyoto, but Edo was the seat of political power. It was required that each feudal daimyo spend part of each year in the city to serve the shogun, for it had become the unofficial national capital by the 1600's. This regular invasion of Edo by the rural leaders and their entourages spurred economic development, and Tokugawa invited merchants and artisans to his city to serve the needs of the growing population. By 1700, with a population of over a million, Edo may have been the largest city on the globe.

Growth of a merchant class in Edo led to many changes in Japanese society. Strict segregation of social classes resulted in the development of a distinct artisan community. There was money and power here, and a mercantile class emerged that enjoyed both making and spending money. Under the patronage of business, Japanese arts such as kabuki theatre and the geisha profession flourished.

It was the arrival of the West, when American Commodore Perry sailed into Tokyo Bay in 1853, that spelled the beginning of the end of Shogunate Japan. The military forces of the country were unable to repel the "Southern Barbarians," and a coalition of powerful Japanese families took advantage of this lapse of power to seize control and restore the Emperor. In 1868, power was again vested in the Emperor. The official capital was moved from Kyoto to Edo, the Emperor settled into Edo Castle, and the name of the city was changed to Tokyo, meaning "Eastern Capital."

Emperor Meiji gave his name to a period of unprecedented economic growth in Japan. The year of his ascendancy, 1868, is an important date in Japanese history. It marks the end of old shogunate Japan and the beginning of the introduction of modern, and western, ideas. Meiji realized early on that the best way to preserve Japanese sovereignty was to cooperate with the western powers. Things western were analyzed, and if deemed superior to those in Japan, were adopted. As a result, the face of Tokyo began to change as western-style red brick buildings rose on sites cleared of wooden Japanese homes.

This period of change in Japanese society was unprecedented. Not only did the face of the nation change, but there was also social, political, and economic upheaval. Never in history had such an enormous reversal of national attention occurred without a war, yet the Japanese people adapted the changes introduced to their centuries-old culture. What made the sweeping changes so orderly was that Japanese society was sophisticated and well-disciplined. Years of homogeneity under the shogunate prepared the population to accept both modern thought and westernization, and to make use of its well-developed political and mercantile skills in a more contemporary environment.

By 1920 the population had risen to over two million, but a disastrous earthquake in 1923 leveled much of what had been built since restoration. Tokyo rebuilt rapidly, however, and by 1932 the population reached four million in the downtown area and the surrounding suburbs.

Japan's relationship with the West was shattered with the onset of World War II. It is unnecessary to present a litany of the horrors of that war, but it is important to reflect on the speed with which we mended our fences following armistice. The American occupation of Japan began when the war ended in 1945 and continued until 1952. General Douglas MacArthur and his staff virtually ran the country, believing that the Japanese government was too feudal, too backward to meet the needs of the modern nation that the Americans had on the drawing board. The same factors which carried the population through the adjustments of the Meiji period hastened the adoption of these post-war changes.

Sweeping reforms were put through, a new constitution written, and existing trade cartels scrapped. Many of the American decisions were unsuited to the realities of life in Japan. But overall, the Americans made an effective occupation force, and they left behind them little resentment on the part of the defeated Japanese. What they did leave behind was a respect for American democracy and an appreciation that the Japanese were treated as equal partners in the future rather than as foes to be severely punished.

One must look beyond Tokyo's history, past its current role as economic and political heartbeat of Japan, and into its narrow back streets and its energetic population to understand why the city is as it is. In spite of its confused and chaotic facade, Tokyo is a city that works, perhaps more efficiently than any other major capital in the world. While in the West we build monuments to the future, in Tokyo people build for the present, and concentrate on making what is current function.

Japanese wedding at Mt. Fuji

Hie Jinja Shrine

Three generations of an Asakusa family

Traditional dancer, Nikko

BACKGROUND

In the opinion of many westerners, Tokyo is just like New York. Simply ask anyone who has never been there and, in a tone indicating expertise, he will say, "Nothing but high-rise hotels, neon signs, and traffic—just like New York."

The Japanese capital does share many traits with the Big Apple. Parts of Tokyo do look startlingly like Times Square. But there is one major difference: Tokyo is the bastion of Japanese, not American society. No matter how western Tokyo may appear it is still a Japanese city in its soul, a city so different from New York that no one who has ever been there could harbor that age-old misconception.

Tokyo is the political and cultural vortex of this nation of four islands, just off the coast of mainland Asia. Not much larger than California, Japan has always been an isolated nation. Less than a third of the land is arable, yet the country is able to support a population of 120 million.

Tokyo has drawn well over eleven million people to join its progress, thirty million if one counts the suburbs. The bustle of Tokyoites, combined with the traffic flow of buses, cars, and trucks, and the quick pace in general accounts for many visitors' initial impressions of a city in constant, sweeping motion through both space and time.

Yet assumptions made at face value often lead to inaccurate judgements about Tokyo society. It is impossible to understand Tokyo without understanding the rubrics which control it. With its huge population, the city's resources, its hygienic and public services, its very space, are stretched beyond what would be considered acceptable in most of the rest of the world.

In spite of this, a position in the government or with one of a handful of major Japanese firms headquartered in Tokyo is still the goal most Japanese parents espouse for their offspring, even though it means living in Tokyo. How have the people adjusted to life in the national capital, or more important, why have they compromised much that was respected in the past in exchange for a high-pressure life of constant work? Given a backdrop as confusing, as hectic as Tokyo, how has Japan managed to rise from its World War II ashes to a position as international economic power?

As their capital has evolved with an eye towards both the past and the future, so have the Japanese themselves. Modern Japanese are surrounded by both the old and the new, and the mutual existence of both tells much about why things are the way they are in Japan. Example: The national religion, Shintoism, has adapted itself neatly to the twentieth century, as have its adherents. Shrines, with fresh offerings of fruits and rice cakes, top many Tokyo skyscrapers. Shinto priests show up to banish evil spirits from the foundations of towering glass-and-steel office buildings. Priests even performed religious rites over the newly-installed kitchen at the 1964 Tokyo Olympic Village before the international athletes were served their first meals. Throbbing gongs break through the cacophony of the traffic from time to time and tiny Shinto shrines seem to elbow their way to the sidewalk in otherwise unbroken facades of offices and shops. The people of Tokyo, Shintoists and Buddhists, Christians and pagans, cannot help but feel the old gods all around them.

Not only the ancient gods, but many of the old social practices that guided Japanese life have survived, albeit in different form. Japan has always been an insular society. For centuries her leaders avoided contact with anything non-Japanese, and even today foreign visitors feel solitary and apart, separated from an understanding of what they see around them by an invisible social wall.

Japanese are superb hosts, and will go out of their way to meet visitors' everyday requests. Casual meetings often lead to carefully-planned excursions, and strangers stop to offer unsolicited guidance. But all the while the foreign visitor has a sense of having intruded upon a family party.

For as trite as it may sound, Japan is in many senses a large family. As a family would, Japanese society expects conformity to rules and customs, and steadfast adherence to goals set out by years of tradition. Individuals are controlled by a family-like arrangement within village structures, even in a city the size of Tokyo. The Japanese have used their age-old skill for turning work and political situations into family relations, enlarging them to meet modern needs. The corporation has itself become sort of a family-village, demanding loyalty to the corporate leaders and their mercantile goals. When questioned about their professional futures, new recruits at Sony, Mitsubishi, Toyota, or any other Japanese mega-business reply that they exist to serve their employer and to follow the guidelines put forth by their corporate parents.

The socialization starts at about the age of three, when competition for entrance into the nation's finest kindergartens begins. Kyoiku Mamas (education mothers) live to drill their children in lessons designed to help them reach the first rung in Japanese corporate ladders. Those who are fortunate enough to get admittance to the top juku (after-school cram classes) and eventually the most respected schools can look forward to a life of security in a business group much like the family. Each person has a niche to fill, a rank informally attached to his name, and the security that goes along with this makes the compromises worthwile.

Concessions to life in Tokyo are extreme. Half a million dollars may buy, if one is lucky enough to find one, a "2DK" flat in downtown Tokyo—two rooms with a dining-kitchen combination. Driving ranges stretch across the rooftops of highrises

Girl Scouts, Imperial Palace Park

Buddhist Elders, Asakusa Omikoshi Festival

Worker returning home, northern suburbs

School children, Asakusa

looking like giant pigeon coops, even though a day out on a public course costs over a hundred dollars. Even the wealthiest of Japan's executives can only think fondly of the gardens they remember from childhood but cannot begin to afford now that they have reached a plateau in life for which they have constantly striven.

Some are just now beginning to question these strongly-inculcated values, and much of what the Japanese are now experiencing sounds familiar in the West. A small number of young people, too young to remember the tragedies of the war years and the imperial rule of the early 1900's, rebel from age-old ethics. They are willing to work hard, but expect as a reward to be able to play hard. Families are vastly more affluent than in pre-war years. Japanese women are slowly changing their traditional roles as well. Though most still choose to stay at home and raise the children (and certainly stay home in the evenings while their husbands entertain in the night spots of Akasaka and Ginza), many are entering Japanese industry and rising to positions of authority. All this is part of Japan's development as a cosmopolitan—not an insular—international capital.

Japanese society is precisely organized and the result is superb service. Things are neat, clean, and orderly. The precision can be frustrating, for it makes it difficult to make even what seem to be the simplest policy changes. But one thing can be said about the huge city: Tokyo works.

This is apparent from the time one first steps onto Japanese soil. Luggage is delivered quickly and in perfect order. The public transportation from the airport is on schedule. The bellboy at the hotel removes your baggage and takes it to your room while refusing a tip. Tipping is looked upon as degrading.

Beyond the sights, the neon, and the temples, there is a spirit of Japan that keeps Tokyo running so smoothly. The people have come to terms with their culture and their environment. Everywhere the traffic hurtles with an unusual kind of abandon. The speed is hectic, but there is an unspoken understanding that everyone is going in the right direction. The pell-mell lifestyle is ablaze with smiles, however, for the Japanese smile with every welcome, every adieu, at every social occasion. Even the smallest social niceties are meticulously followed, for this is a land in which form is often more important than function. The easy, casual compatibility of the West, the way in which we are quick to address a new acquaintance by his or her given name is alien to Japanese society.

Ceremony is a everyday part of life in Tokyo, either in a social or a business setting. The rubrics of society may not be set down on paper, but are clearly understood by Japanese from all walks of life. A professional meeting is never held in a private office, for example, but more likely in a reception room especially for the purpose. An office is a place to work, perhaps more personal and private than a generic meeting room. Nor does the meeting get underway without elaborate introductions and polite, non-business conversation. The ritual is as important to the Japanese as the practical topics of the meeting. It establishes an equality and reminds the participants that the Japanese corporation is not just brick-and-mortar, but a collection of dedicated people.

This proscribed ceremony can be exasperating, but it marks the distinction between Japanese "formalists" and western "functionalists." How business is done is as important as the fact that it is done at all. Though progress seems slower, relationships are cemented that weather commercial storms and breach even the most serious trade disagreements.

In a nation so jam-packed with people it is a blessing that the social graces are so well practiced. People wait politely in lines for buses and obey traffic crossing signals without question. They conform to the rules—both written and unwritten—that guide the massive city and its millions of residents through daily life in what could otherwise be very frustating circumstances. In other countries, the rate of crime always increases as the quality of life improves. But in Japan, exactly the opposite is true. Tokyo averages less than one percent the number of robberies as New York. Visitors routinely leave valuables unlocked in hotel rooms safe in the knowledge that they will be there when they return.

Many find the graciousness, the smiles, and the manners a bit disarming at first, but they are but charming adjustments to life in the world's busiest, most densely-populated city. The visitor who allows the surface drabness and the hectic pace to dominate his feeling about the Japanese capital misses all that is vibrant and vital. Conversely, the westerner who thinks that he can ever completely understand Japan, who thinks that he can ever be completely accepted in its society is probably going to be disappointed. But he who scratches the surface, who looks deeper than the shop windows and the train station crowds will be rewarded. He who cannot will come away agreeing with everything he heard at home: Tokyo is just like New York.

Ginza and Hamamatsucho, from Toyomi across Tokyo Harbor

OVERVIEW OF CITY

From Tokyo Tower, the city's "Eiffel," Tokyo looks like a single vast entity. It is indeed an immense city. But its individual neighborhoods are so diverse as to suggest that the huge metropolis is really nothing more than a collection of different towns and villages, one of the reasons for its vitality. Many were indeed separate villages until they were gradually absorbed as Tokyo's boundaries bulged in every direction. Each of Tokyo's commercial and governmental hubs has, within a stone's throw, a network of narrow back streets where life goes on seemingly oblivious to the daily pace nearby.

It is this contrast of old Japan—new Japan, the face Tokyo typically puts on for the West vs. that which she quietly preserves for her sons and daughters that makes the city so exhilarating. Her neighborhoods reflect the dichotomy of Tokyo perfectly. Surprises literally await around each corner. Historically, it begins in Tokyo's oldest neighborhood, the area around the Imperial Palace where the shoguns first established the castle-town that became the city of Tokyo.

The Imperial Palace, built by the first Edo Shogun, is Tokyo's birthplace. The original buildings were destroyed during World War II, but the moats and many of the Imperial bridges remain. The Nijubashi double bridge was the front gate of the castle of the Emperor Meiji and is now the main entrance to the modern palace. Its graceful arch and carved stonework is straight from Japan's classical past.

Four of the original Edo Palace gates stand in the East garden. Cherry trees line the moats. The main palace is closed to visitors, but sightseers and natives alike relax beneath the gnarled Japanese black pines. Groups gather noisily at Nijubashi to take family pictures with the famous bridge in the background.

Just west of the Imperial Palace is Marunouchi. The tree-lined streets of Marunouchi are straight and orderly, and its skyscrapers give the quarter a businesslike uniformity. The offices and boardrooms, deep inside the multi-story towers, still control the heartbeat of industrial Japan. Tokyo Station is the focal point of Marunouchi, and the point of departure for the famous Bullet trains going to the south of Japan.

At the end of the last century, Marunouchi, once the home of the Shogun's samurai, had decayed and was known as "Gambler's Field." The land was purchased by the Mitsubishi Company, already an economic force in Japan with which to be reckoned. Within twenty-five years a development of English-style office buildings had sprung up. After World War II, the early Mitsubishi buildings were razed in favor of today's multi-story skyscrapers and the corporate personality continued unabated.

The corporate giants of Marunouchi often turn their attention to nearby Nihombashi, once a center of artisans and craftsmen and now the city's financial soul. Even during the Edo period there was great wealth here, some of the elaborate residences of samurai line the banks of the Sumida River.

Outwardly, little remains from these early days. There are a handful of Edo-era shops and some red brick of the Meiji period. What does survive is the conservatism of the ancient financiers, and the dignity that has always surrounded banking.

After the official close of business many of Japan's executives move to the restaurants and night clubs of Ginza to continue their negotiations. Ginza at night is a chic entertainment center, brightly-lit by thousands of colorful neon signs. "Gin" means silver, and "za" identifies a licensed group of craftsmen, the name coming to the village after the Shogun's silver mint was moved here in 1612.

Today, the name "Ginza" is almost synonymous with shopping. The area is so linked with retailing that stores and shops named Ginza have sprung up all over the world. Branches of every major Japanese department store can be found in Ginza, some with direct access to their basement showrooms from the subway.

Nearby Tsukiji is home for the Tokyo Central Wholesale Market, where the day begins early. It is one of the largest and most modern markets in the world. Fish, as well as vegetables and other commodities are sold here at spirited auctions.

There is history and culture in Tsukiji as well. Hama Detached Palace Garden was once the favorite duck-hunting grounds of the Shoguns, the site of an early imperial villa. It is laid out in the traditional Japanese manner, with water on three sides and narrow paths winding around several placid ponds.

Shiba is south and west of Ginza. When the early shoguns planned Edo they set aside land here for Zojoji Temple. The temple was placed at one of the city's southern gates, as much a religious place as a first level of defense for Edo's occupants. The original temple dates from the 1400's, though the hall that stands on the spot now is a post-war reconstruction. Only the 1605 gate remains from the Edo period.

The park is a stark contrast to the old temple gate. There is a golf driving range which would surely seem incongruous to the Tokugawa Shoguns. At the edge of the green expanse stands Tokyo Tower, the Japanese equivalent to Paris' Eiffel Tower. There is an observation platform 836 feet above Tokyo which gives a breathtaking view of the Japanese capital.

Hamamatsucho, like Shiba is a hotel center, with quiet residential streets and old shops that sell traditional Japanese wares. Tokyo's World Trade Center, home to many consulates and shipping firms has an extraordinary view of Tokyo from its pinnacle. Hamamtsucho is also one of Tokyo's thriving port areas.

Shimbasi changed its personality as progress changed Tokyo's transportation patterns. The opening of Tokyo Station left Shimbasi moored in the past. Once one of the two greatest geisha districts in the city, after the opening of the new rail station the shops and entertainment centers moved to Ginza.

The government center of Tokyo and of all of Japan is in Kasumigaseki, north of Shiba and near the Palace District Parliament meets in the National Diet Building. Completed in 1936, its tower is one of the city's main landmarks. In a small park near the Diet Building is the Tomb of the Unknown Soldiers, built in 1959 to the memory of those who died in the "Great Pacific War."

Nearby is the Ministry of Foreign Affairs, many embassies including that of the

Shinjuku East

Students in front of a statue of Ota Dokan

Omikoshi Festival, Tsukiji

Tourists in Nikko

United States, and several modern hotels. In the middle of this bureaucratic center is the ancient Hie Jinja Shrine, built by Edo's first ruler, Ota Dokan. The shrine is one of the oldest historic sites in the city, having been moved to its present site in 1659.

Kasumigaseki and Hibya merge in modern Tokyo, though centuries ago there were distinct differences. Hibya, like Ginza, was once marshland wrested from the sea by the Shoguns and is noted for Hibya Park, the vortex of the area. Daimyo castles occupied much of the village, and after the restoration of the Emperor in 1868 the Meiji ruler purposely turned Hibya into a government and diplomatic area.

"Roppongi" means "six trees," one theory suggesting that it recalls six samurai who lived here during the days of the Shogunates. After the re-establishment of the Imperial government, Roppongi became the home of wealthy Japanese and foreign embassy workers. Embassies continued to locate here after World War II, and Roppongi slowly became an enclave for foreign residents of Tokyo.

Not long ago, but a single streetcar line served Roppongi, and shops served only local residents. Today, Roppongi's streets are lined with European cinemas and small reasonable restaurants. Rock music spills from open doorways into the crowds on the sidewalks. The international flavor of the neighborhood, which had been long established, attracted western style bars and restaurants in the 1950's and 1960's and the young Japanese nouveau-riche were attracted to Roppongi.

Roppongi sights usually revolve around some sort of leisure pursuit. The major landmark is the multi-story pink coffeehouse, Almond, at Roppongi Crossing. The Square Building houses seven discos in its ten stories. The actions seems non-stop in Roppongi, the neon flashing until the wee small hours long after the rest of Tokyo has called it a day.

Among Tokyo's neighborhoods are several glittering, enormous neon jewels. Akasaka is the most sophisticated, perhaps the most expensive of these areas that seem to take on a new identity after the sun goes down. During the day it is quiet and traditional. Tiny shops on narrow back streets sell kimonos, fans, and Japanese dolls. The alleys wind their way among wide boulevards not unlike the Champs Elysees. After sunset the pace quickens in Akasaka, but the clientele is different from that in nearby Roppongi. This is an expense-account district, and the deluxe accommodations at Akasaka's luxury hotels cater to business and political interests.

The Japanese style buildings of uniform sand hues lining Akasaka's side streets are home to the most famed of Japanese "ryotei" restaurants, where the finest of traditional Japanese cuisine is served by the silk-robed geishas. A foreigner should indeed feel flattered to be invited to dine here, where many of the most important business and political relationships in Japan are forged.

Tokyo's fashion center, Aoyama, is to the west of Akasaka. The main drag through the section is Aoyama-Dori, a curious street that has remnants of old Japan tucked between modern western shops. There are sophisticated boutiques and stores with elegant, expensive silk kimonos next to tiny shops filled with tea caddies and handleless Japanese porcelain cups. Italiàn, Korean, Chinese, and Japanese restaurants sit amicably beside Parisian bistros.

Life moves at a hectic, sophisticated pace. Architecture reflects the influence of the West. The Akasaka Detached Palace, a state guest house, resembles Buckingham Palace on the exterior and Versailles once one has passed through the doors. Aoyama Twin Towers, built in 1969, is startling in its western sophistication.

Shibuya is another high fashion district that radiates from Shibuya Station. Streets fan out in all directions from the station, windows filled with youthful clothing and accessories. Colors vie for one's attention, and a shopping trip to Shibuya can be both exciting and tiring.

Harajuku is undoubtedly the Picadilly Circus of Tokyo, a magnet that draws what surely must be every resident of Tokyo under the age of twenty-five each evening. These are Japan's spoiled kids, the children of post-war prosperity. Cheap copies of the designer apparel that is shown in Aoyama fill Harajuku windows, and the crowds in the streets are testimony to the dedication of Japanese youth to the endless pursuit of fashion.

Nearby Yoyogi Park is a popular meeting place for Tokyo teens and at the same time the site of the city's most important temple, the Meiji Shrine. The park was home to the 1964 Tokyo Olympic Village and is thickly-wooded, the trees having been donated by individuals all over Japan.

Meiji Shrine, in Yoyogi, was completed in 1920 in honor of the Emperor Meiji, who returned Imperial rule to Japan in 1868. Meiji is the "Holy of Holies" for Japanese Buddhists, their most important religious site. Torii Gates, large symbolic wooden structures, arch over the entrances to the Inner Garden, with its impressive iris beds, water lily pond, and traditional tea house. The Shrine is in the Inner Garden, and is the destination of over a million Japanese pilgrims each year.

Shinjuku, north of Shibuya, was once a small crossroads town. Most natives knew it only for the busy coach station which was an important gateway to the rest of Japan. The hub of modern Shinjuku is still a station—but today it is for the train and not for horse-drawn coaches. Two million people pass through Shinjuku Station daily, making it maybe the largest station in the world.

While Shinjuku has grown along with the rest of Tokyo, it has managed to retain a bit of its traditional role in Tokyo life. During the days of the Shoguns, or so the story goes, a disagreement between the son of a prominent samurai and the owner of a local brothel led to the destruction of the area. By the end of the nineteenth century Shinjuku was again notorious for its wall-to-wall houses of prostitution.

Today the area is divided geographically and socially. The Kabukicho section of east Shinjuku is often compared to Times Square in New York. Inexpensive restaurants stand between movie houses and sex shops. East Shinjuku is hardly recognizable as the rice-paddy crossroads that it was just a century ago.

West Shinjuku, in contrast, is Tokyo's up-and-coming business address. It is here that you will find the newest, most sumptuous hotels. Japan's economic wealth is displayed in dozens of skyscrapers whose designs and amenities are among the world's most modern.

Sunshine Sixty, at 787 feet and Tokyo's tallest building, towers above Ikebukuro,

Asakusa children in traditional costume

Grand Palace Hotel

Aoyama, a western-style fashion center

A small restaurant in Asakusa

a Tokyo neighborhood in transition. Once primarily a working-class area, it is rapidly becoming an important shopping and entertainment district.

Sunshine City epitomizes the newest trends here. It is a complex of four buildings, housing a hotel, space for international exhibits, theatres, art galleries, and a large variety of shops and restaurants. Its towering Sunshine Sixty building alone has a ground floor area of 15 acres.

Ueno's shops once catered to the city's craftsmen and workers. Her flower pot-lined streets and alleys, more than in any other Tokyo neighborhood, still reflect life in the Japanese capital in the mid-1800's.

Each spring, when the cherry blossoms come to life, millions flock to Ueno Park, the centerpiece of the neighborhood. Its 131 acres are famous not only for the fabulous cherry blossoms, but also for the lotus blooms on Shinobazu Pond that draw thousands every day.

The name of Ueno dates to 1631, when Kaneiji Temple covered the entire park. Today, only the 5-story pagoda, Goju No Too, remains. Nearby is Toshogu Shrine, built in honor of the first Tokugawa Shogun. Ueno has two other important religious buildings. Benzaiten Temple is set on a small island. Nearby Gojoten Temple is isolated in the woods. The setting is quiet and peaceful, reminiscent of the times when Tokyo was but a small village.

It is these reminders of the past that make Ueno so charming. Country people fill its streets, arriving from the North at Ueno Station, home of the Bullet trains going to the north of Japan. Many shops and restaurants remain from the Edo period to cater to the non-city dwellers, giving Ueno much of its old-fashioned feeling.

While some Tokyo neighborhoods have fled their past as the city moved into the twentieth century others, the "shitamachi," were able to adapt to the new and at the same time retain much of their old flavor. One of these, Asakusa, epitomizes the old merchant-artisan areas and has prospered as the gateway to the Sensoji Temple for 300 years. Like many other old towns, Asakusa has been absorbed by Tokyo and has greatly changed.

Yet Asakusa reflects more of the old character than any other Tokyo neighborhood. It was a mercantile center during the Meiji period, but when the railroads became the city's most important mode of transportation, little Asakusa Station remained a minor stop. The environment was rural well into the 1900's.

The focal point here is still Sensoji Temple, the entrance to which is a gaily-lit shopping street filled with souvenir shops. The temple, dedicated to the Buddhist God of Mercy, is Tokyo's oldest. Thousands visit there daily, many coming to worship at the ancient altar. The garden was laid out by a master of Japanese garden art, and the elaborate gates to the temple area have stood since the time of the Shoguns.

The real reason for coming to Asakusa, however, is to wander. Craftsmen still work in old shops in the traditional way, and ancient Japanese culture is an everyday part of life. The little shops offer goods found nowhere else in Tokyo. There are lots of places to sip coffee and watch the passersby, and little fear of boredom in this old Japanese area.

Just behind Asakusa Station, the Sumida River flows through Asakusabashi, a neighborhood of small office buildings and apartments as well as a generations-old fishing fleet. Gardens and parks line both sides of the river, and offer pleasant places for strolling.

Many come to Asakusabashi to buy the popular Japanese dolls. The geisha dolls, whose finely-crafted features are surprisingly life-like, reflect life here a hundred years ago. The "Willow Bridge" which crosses the Kanda River here was famous as a geisha quarter during the Meiji years and a few "ryotel," geisha restaurants, remain today.

For electronics, the best place in town is Akihibara, between Ueno and Tokyo Station. Stores are piled high with stereo equipment, computers, appliances, tape recorders, video gear, and virtually anything that you can plug into the wall.

Akihibara means "Autumn leaf fields," but the fields are long gone. The spectacle is of thousands of TV screens, some no larger than a thumbnail, blasting out "Doctor Kildaire" dubbed in Japanese or the play-by-play of the Yomiuri Giants vs. the Chunichi Dragons in the bottom of the ninth.

Casual visitors to Tokyo, those who are unable or unwilling to let down their western stereotypes of life in the world's most densely-populated city, cannot appreciate the energy nor the spirit that keeps Tokyo plugging along. Granted, it is difficult if not impossible to pick a point where one neighborhood that was once an ancient village becomes another neighborhood with an equally-long history. Everything that is or ever was Japanese merges along the wide boulevards, yet on the side streets the delineation between real Japan and westernized Japan becomes plain.

Few cities on earth have been able to maintain any small-town ambiance at all in the face of the demands of progress. New York has Harlem and Greenwich Village perhaps, and these are physical symbols of lifestyles long since abandoned. But in neither case does one find residents who cling to tradition as to those of Ueno or Asakusa. Tokyo may not have saved her physical history, as much of the old architecture has been taken by earthquake or war regardless of the best of Japanese intentions. What she has saved, however, in her narrow corners and twisted alleys, is the humanity of Japan.

Imperial Palace, Statue of Ota Dokan

IMPERIAL PALACE

In the 15th Century, a minor Shogun, Ota Dokan, built a castle town called Edo. The small village prospered, and the local economy expanded in response to the needs of the Lord and his samurai. Three hundred years later, Edo became Tokyo after the restoration of the Emperor to power.

Imperial Palace

Only the gates remain of the original Imperial Palace, all the other buildings having been destroyed in World War II. Surrounding the palace are the remains of the Edo Castle moats and three Japanese gardens.

Tokyo Station, Marunouchi

MARUNOUCHI

TOKYO STATION Meiji-era brick buildings form the core of the Tokyo Station which was built in 1914. Today, the station is the home of the famous Shinkasen, or "Bullet" trains going south and west.

Marunouchi

MARUNOUCHI Most major Japanese corporations are headquartered in Marunouchi, which has come to be Japan's most prestigious commercial address. Since the earliest days of the Meiji Restoration trade and business have been carried on here, and when Tokyo Station was located here the importance of Marunouchi was strengthened.

Nihombashi

NIHOMBASHI

NIHOMBASHI Showadori Avenue is the main boulevard through this financial area. Nihombashi has been the banking center of Japan since the Edo period, and is today the headquarters of most important Japanese financial concerns, including the Bank of Japan and the Bank of Tokyo. In 1896, the Bank of Japan opened its headquarters in Nihombashi. The bank was joined by stock traders and other financial enterprise, and today the Tokyo Stock Exchange, the world's largest, is in Nihombashi.

Bank of Tokyo, Nihombashi

Ginza

GINZA

The names of many important Japanese companies—NEC, Fujiya, and others—are immortalized in the neon of Ginza. Modern Ginza is Tokyo's most famous shopping area, with hundreds of fashionable (and expensive) boutiques and department stores.

Ginza

Harumi-Dori Avenue is one of Ginza's busiest shopping streets. At night, restaurants and clubs advertise in the flashy neon that has, in part, become the neighborhood's hallmark.

Ginza

The streets of Ginza are crowded day and night. Shoppers throng Ginza thoroughfares during the day, having visited some of Tokyo's most exclusive shops. At night, Tokyo businessmen come here, often on their expense accounts, and business relationships are forged over the dining tables of Ginza.

Mitsukoshi Department Store, Ginza

The classic Japanese department store, Mitsukoshi opened in 1673 as a kimono shop. It was the first Japanese store to add a second floor and glass display cases. Mitsukoshi still has the city's largest selection of kimonos and other Japanese goods.

Tokyo Wholesale Market, Tsukiji

TSUKIJI

Tokyo's main fish market is located in this off-beat tourist area near Ginza. Buying and selling starts before the sun comes up, and the area is dotted with seafood restaurants that offer, of course, the freshest fish in town. Experts agree that the best sushi in Tokyo can be found here.

Hama Rikyu Gardens, Tsukiji

The garden in Tsukiji, around a former Tokugawa shogun's villa, is a good example of the life of the wealthy during the Edo period. It centers around a pond, and has three bridges covered with wisteria vines.

Tokyo Tower at night

World Trade Center, Hamamatsucho

SHIBA/HAMAMATSUCHO/SHIMBASHI

Two of Tokyo's tallest towers are near each other south of the Imperial Palace. Tokyo Tower is a model of the Eiffel Tower in Paris, except it is 100 feet taller than its French counterpart. The World Trade Center, in Hamamatsucho, was built in 1970.

Zojoji Temple, Shiba

Zojoji was a Tokugawa family tower built to protect the Imperial Palace from the south. This is the third temple on this site, descending from the first structure built in 1393. The main gate, from 1605, is the only building that remains from the Edo period.

Shimbashi

Shimbashi has always been in the shadow of its more prosperous and more well-known neighbor, Ginza. During the Meiji period, Shimbashi was known as a second-rate geisha quarter, and after the Meiji restoration in 1868 the streets soon filled with cheap shops and drinking spots.

Shiba

Modern Shiba begins on the street just outside the Zojoji Temple. Once one of Tokyo's leading ports, when reclamation projects set Shiba back from the sea coast the merchants moved to neighboring Hamamatsucho.

The Japanese Supreme Court, Kasumagaseki

KASUMAGASEKI

A government office district, Kasumagaseki is home to the National Diet Building, the Prime Minister's residence, and a host of ministeries. Japan's first skyscraper, the 36-story Kasumagaseki Building, was built here in 1968.

The National Diet Building, Kasumagaseki

Large and very official looking, the National Diet Building was completed in 1936. Japan's Parliament meets here. The building is topped by a pyramidal 236-foot tall tower.

Imperial Hotel from Hibya Park

HIBYA

Hibya was part of the land reclaimed from the sea during the Edo period. The Imperial Hotel, the third hotel on the site, was built in 1968 after a previous building designed by American Frank Lloyd Wright was razed. Hibya is now the home of numerous theatres and movie houses.

Hibya Park garden

Hibya Park was the site of an important daimyo mansion during the Edo years. There are over 200 species of trees on its 41 acres, and the park is known all over Japan for its azaleas and chrysanthemums. Hibya Park is Tokyo's largest western-style garden.

The Almond Coffeehouse, Roppongi

ROPPONGI

The most international area in Tokyo, Roppongi is known for its youthful nightlife. The Almond is a major landmark, and sets the stage for the district's many western style bars, coffee shops, and restaurants. The Square Building, in Roppongi, houses seven discos in a ten-story building.

Roppongi Street

Jazz clubs and discos line the sidewalks in Roppongi. The entertainment palaces here are less expensive than those in Ginza and Akasaka, and the crowds are definitely more blond-haired and blue-eyed. The district claims some of Tokyo's best restaurants and night spots.

AKASAKA
With their children in traditional Japanese costume, this family is posing in front of the Hie Jinja Shrine. In the late 15th century, Ota Dokan built a shrine here, the site of an early castle. The present building dates from 1959.

Aoyami-Dori

The contrasts of Akasaka

Few Tokyo neighborhoods display the stark contrasts of Akasaka. The side streets are lined with Japanese-style buildings that house ryotei, exclusive geisha restaurants. Yet along the wide boulevards, Tokyo's most modern hotels give the district a distinctly twentieth-century appearance.

AOYAMA

Life moves at an expensive, sophisticated pace in Aoyama, one of Tokyo's leading fashion districts. The main street, Aoyama-Dori, is the address for hundreds of boutiques, specialty shops, and restaurants.

Aoyama-Dori Boulevard

The wide boulevards of Aoyama remind some visitors of the Champs Elysees. Like the famous Paris street, Aoyama's boulevards are lined with exclusive shops, the windows filled with expensive, western-style fashions.

Shibuya neon

SHIBUYA

Shibuya is somewhere between the abandon of Harajuku and the nouveau-sophistication of Aoyoma. Like many other Tokyo neighborhoods, there are many boutiques and theatres. Each evening, thousands of young Japanese office workers flock to the discos and the nomiya—Japanese bars.

Shibuya nightlife

Until recently, Shibuya was a quiet residential area. The neighborhood was named after a family of the same name whose castle was located here during the Edo period. Today it is the competing department stores, constantly being updated to keep the customers coming in, that set the pace.

Harajuku shops

Fashions in Harajuku windows

Boutiques and department stores, Harajuku

Harajuku shopping

HARAJUKU

If there is a youth capital of Japan, it certainly must be Harajukyu. Cheap knock-offs of designer fashions that hang in the windows of Aoyama are available in the boutiques of Harajuku. The district swarms with the spoiled children of Japan's economic boom.

Harajuku Street

The streets of Harajuku are clogged with Japan's restless youth. The main landmark is the La Foret fashion building, down the street from one of Tokyo's cheapest shopping areas. Literally tons of clothes, in imitation of popular western styles, spill from closet-sized shops.

Meiji Shrine

MEIJI SHRINE

A garden of over a hundred thousand trees surround the Meiji Shrine in Harajuku. This was a favorite garden of the Meiji Emperor and Empress, where more than 100 varieties of irises bloom in the early summer.

Meiji Shrine

The shrine in Harajuku is a perfect example of refined Shinto religious architecture. This is the center of the Shinto religion in Japan. It is one of the most frequently visited shrines in Tokyo.

Shinjuku West

Shinjuku West

SHINJUKU WEST

Many would call Shinjuku the most vibrant, spirited neighborhood of Tokyo. In its western region, Shinjuku has become an ultra-modern commercial area. Progress in Shinjuku dates from the establishment of the Shinjuku Station in 1889 to serve the western suburbs.

Shinjuku West

Facades in Shinjuku West compete as they rise from the sidewalks. Around the station are some of the highest rents in Japan.

Shinjuku Gyoen Garden

At 150 acres, the Shinjuku Gyoen Garden is formerly the estate of an Edo period daimyo family. The grounds contain a traditional Japanese garden, a formal French garden, and an extensive greenhouse with tropical plants.

Mitsui Building, Shinjuku West

Shinjuku is the home of many of Japan's largest trading companies. These firms are huge conglomerates that reach into every aspect of Japanese commerce, from manufacturing to finance and distribution. The idea of a trading company dates to the Meiji period, and by World War II the companies had already become as sophisticated in their mercantile skills as those in western business centers.

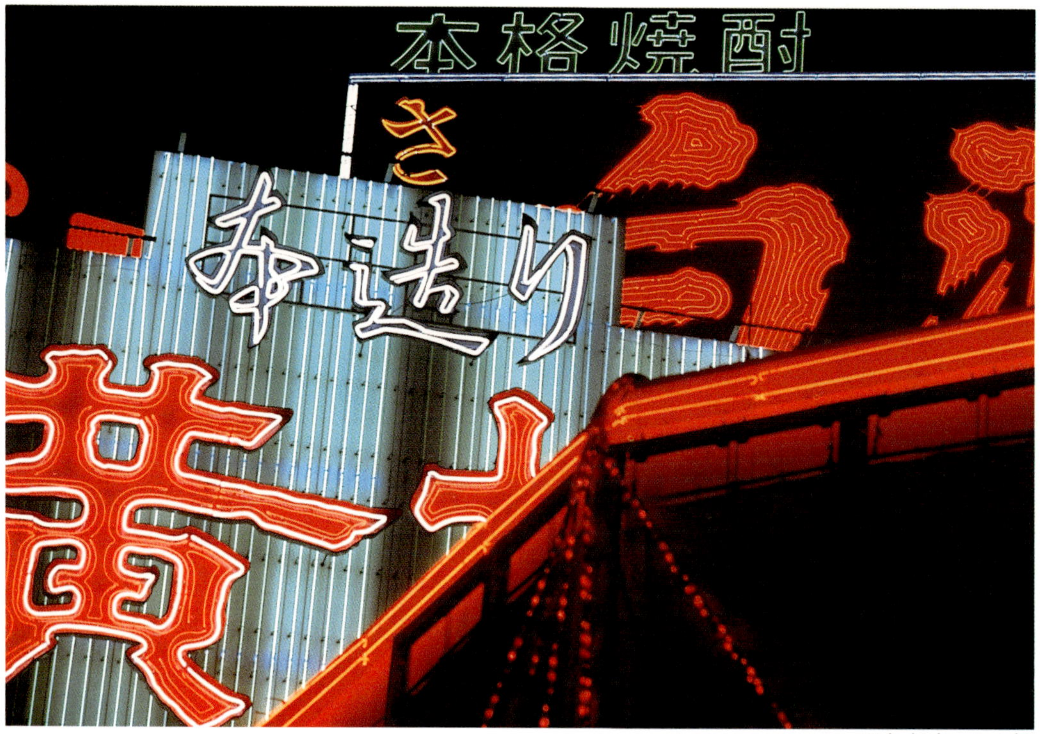

Kabukicho at night

Nightlife, Kabukicho

SHINJUKU EAST/KABUKICHO

After dark, Kabukicho in eastern Shinjuku comes to life. The Kabuki theatre was once the cultural focus of the area, and today the streets are filled with movie houses, coffee houses, and cabarets.

Kabukicho

Kabukicho has a long tradition as a pleasure quarter. The kabuki theatre never succeeded here, but modern Tokyoites come by the thousands nonetheless. The reputation has changed, for Kabukicho is known as Tokyo's "red light" district.

Sunshine City, Ikebukuro

Ikebukuro shopping mall

Dining in Ikebukuro

IKEBUKURO

Until the Meiji period, Ikebukuro was mostly forests and farmlands. Today the enormous Seibu Department Store is not only the largest store in the world, but is also the chief attraction in Ikebukuro. Sunshine City is the tallest building in Asia, at sixty stories high.

Ikebukuro streets

During the 1930's, Ikebukuro was the haunt of Tokyo's renegade artists and writers. Neon flashes over the streets of modern Ikebukuro as crowds fill the sidewalks after dark.

The 5-story Pagoda, Ueno

UENO

Ueno was one of the city's major temple districts during the Edo period. Temples doubled as forts to fend off intruders who would have attacked from the northeast. After the Meiji Restoration in 1868, a few Tokugawa loyalists took over the Ueno temples, and in the ensuing battle the temples were destroyed.

Lotus blossoms on Shinobazu Pond, Ueno park

Ueno Park was the first place in Japan to have a zoo and a museum. Shinobazu Pond, in the western part of the park, was originally marshland. It was annexed to the park in 1885, landscapes, and soon became a favorite spot for viewing water lilies and lotus blooms.

Toshogu Shrine, Ueno

The Tokugawa shoguns were the first of Japan's feudal leaders to forge a national government on the island nation. They did so by forcing the lesser shoguns to their will, and in the process created the city of Edo, which became Tokyo. Six of the Tokugawa shoguns are buried in Ueno. Toshogu Shrine was built in the Chinese style in 1651 in the temple area that became Ueno Park.

Shinobazu Pond, Ueno Park

Ueno Park is popular for all sorts of outdoor activities, including boating on Shinobazu Pond. In 1873, the park became the first public park in Tokyo, and is now a museum center as well as a natural preserve.

Shinobazu Pond, Ueno Park

Ueno Park is the favorite spot in all Tokyo for looking at cherry blossoms, a tradition that goes back to the Tokugawa shoguns. Benzaiten Temple is on a small island in the pond, often surrounded by lotus blossoms.

Ueno Park

Early plans for Ueno, after the defeat of the Tokugawa forces and the arrival of the Emperor in Tokyo, called for the establishment of a medical university on the site. Happily, it was decided to locate the school elsewhere and turn the hilltop into a park.

Sensoji Temple, Asakusa

ASAKUSA

The neighborhood of Asakusa is centered around the Sensjoi Temple, popularly called Asakusa Kannon-dera. Asakusa is one Tokyo neighborhood which, more than any other, retains its Meiji-era atmosphere.

Asakusa, Sensoji Temple

A story tells of two Buddhist Fishermen who found in their nets a statue of Kannon, the goddess of mercy. Sensoji Temple was built as a home to the statue in the seventh century. The present building is a replica built in 1958, following the destruction of an earlier building during World War II.

Asakusa

The centerpiece of Japanese religious festivals is the omikoshi, a portable shrine of a local god that is carried by the faithful during festivals all over the city in the spring and early summer. Some weigh upwards of several tons, requiring the cooperation of many willing shoulders. The procession is accompanied by the beating of the taiko drums and many sacred, and ancient dances.

Asakusa

Participants in the omikoshi parades usually wear costumes from the old Edo period. At the front is often a leader in a grotesque mask, sometimes a dragon, sometimes a lion. The procession winds through the streets of the neighborhood, ending up, in this case, at Sensoji Temple in Asakusa.

Buddhist Elders, Asakusa

Buddhism was imported from China in about 538 AD, and undermined the ancient Shinto religion that was already established there. The new religion became both a political tool and a doctrine for the training of samurai warriors. Buddhism remains alive in modern Japan, though Japanese today are extremely casual about their religion.

Sensoji Temple, Asakusa

Buddhist temples are easily-recognized in Japan because of their extravagant, Chinese-style architecture. At the entrances, the faithful will "wash" themselves in the smoke from huge incense burners in hopes of curing or preventing illness.

Sensoji Temple, Asakusa

A promenade to Sensoji Temple is lined with small shops selling souvenirs and refreshments.
Some have been in the same family for generations.

Streets, Asakusa

Restaurant boats on the Sumida River, Asakusabashi

ASAKUSABASHI/AKIHABARA

Asakusabashi was, years ago, the departure point for boats to the north. Some of the boathouses became ryotei, exclusive geisha restaurants. Today, many of the boats are floating dining spots and night clubs.

Akihabara

Formerly the ground of an Edo period shrine called Akiba, or autumn leaf, modern Akihabara is Tokyo's discount electronics district. The selection of electronic goods is mind-boggling, and such a concentration of distributors makes this a buyer's market.

Temple dogs, Nikko

ARTS AND ENTERTAINMENT

Tokyo's bright neon lights and bustling streets give an impression of a city of little cultural wealth. But there is more than shopping and night life here. The capital city is the artistic heart of the nation, and a major center of culture and the arts.

Japan is a nation that takes its art seriously, and the people see art in many more facets of life than we do in the West. Form is very important in this island nation, often more important than function. It is not the fact that a thing has been done but the fashion in which it has been accomplished that can guide a person's priorities. In this regard it is difficult to separate art from life, for not only is Japan's art represented in her museums and galleries, but also in the Sumo ring, the tea ceremony, and even daily business negotiations. In the west there is a saying: "He has made an art" of something or the other. In Japan, everything has been made an art of.

Like nearly every other aspect of Tokyo life, the arts have been twisted and changed by influences from the outside. The earliest forces were from China, by way of Korea, where some believe that virtually everything Japanese began.

By the beginning of the rule of the Tokugawa Shoguns Japan had begun to seal herself off from the outside world. This allowed native artists to gradually develop art forms unique to Japan, "ukiyoe," or people's art. This usually takes the form of paintings, watercolor being the preferred medium. After the introduction of Buddhism to Japan in the sixth century, paintings of religious subjects began to appear. As demand for Japanese art grew, artists turned to decorating folding screens and the sliding doors of paper that are so typical of traditional Japanese architecture.

Following the political changes of 1868, western styles began to creep into the work of Japanese artists, and the western influence is still predominant today. The scope of what can be legitimately called art has expanded also to include fashion design and striking patterns of applied art.

In Japan, like in much of the rest of the eastern world, art and literature are made almost inseparable by the calligraphy that usually accompanies a painting. Many would argue that poetry is the basis of all Japanese art forms, including fine arts, applied and decorative arts, and even performing arts. The grace and beauty of the Chinese ideographs (characters) that descend down one or the other side of a scroll painting can be appreciated even by someone with no knowledge of the written language. Many Japanese entrances feature a horizontal scroll painting, a "makemono," while the "kakemono," or vertical painting, is reserved for the best room and accompanied by a flower arrangement.

In the early seventeenth century the first Japanese woodblock prints were made, an art which flourishes today and which can be within the range of even the humblest budget. The prints of the Edo period, however, are actively sought by collectors around the world and can go well into six figures.

It is difficult to draw a line between Japanese arts and Japanese crafts, for much of the creative energy of one can easily be observed in the other. Craft is more accessible, however, largely because more of the tradition of Japanese craft has remained unchanged. There are still villages where most of the population makes pottery in ancient styles, decorative bamboo items, or the popular Japanese "kokeshi" dolls. Skilled craftsmen have been dubbed "National Treasures" for their work, much as an important building may become a registered landmark.

As in the fine arts, much of Japanese craft has a strong Chinese influence. Local ceramics can be found all over Japan as well as in the galleries which specialize in ceramics in Tokyo. The shapes of the pots and the glazes the potters use have definite links to China.

Contemporary art has lagged a bit behind in Japan. While her graphic arts are well-recognized and appear in glitzy magazines around the globe, innovative art for its own sake has never been wholeheartedly embraced. Two veins of modern art dominate the work done in Japan, both essentially old fashioned. The first is ink and water color paintings in traditional styles, always good-sellers in the hundreds of Tokyo galleries frequented by foreign visitors. The second is a more western style, close to that of the early French impressionists.

Ueno Park is Tokyo's home of the visual arts, being the greatest concentration of important museums in the city. The Tokyo Metropolitan Festival Hall, in Ueno Park, is a striking blend of early Japanese styles and modern architecture.

Tokyo National Museum is built upon a core of Japanese artworks: extensive collections of lacquerware, paintings, sculptures, textiles, and ceramics. One of its four buildings houses the Gallery of Eastern Antiquities. The Tokyo National Museum is the largest museum in Japan and houses the nation's most impressive collection of Japanese art and archaeology.

Nearby is the National Museum of Western Art, whose collection includes 50 works by Rodin and canvasses by Cezanne, Monet, Degas, and other French Impressionists. Next door is the National Science Museum, with everything from Egyptian mummies to steam locomotives. The Tokyo Municipal Museum of Art has collected nearly a thousand pieces of Japanese artwork. On the edge of Ueno Park, the Tokyo University of the Arts spotlights native artists in frequent displays.

Museum and gallery building has become almost a fad in Tokyo in recent years. In addition to the prominent collections already noted, there are dozens of other museums, some built around the collections of wealthy individuals or corporations. The Nezu Art Museum, in Ueno, is especially proud of a vast collection of screen paintings of irises on gold. In the southwestern suburbs of Tokyo, the Goto Museum is one of the city's most comprehensive collections of Chinese art. All told, well over a hundred museums display virtually every aspect of life in both ancient and modern Japan.

What is artistic in Japan, even if one limits oneself to the visually artistic, is not always gallery-oriented. "Ikebana," the world-famous art of Japanese flower-arranging, is every bit as much an art form as is ink painting. Several schools of flower arranging sprung from the Silver Pavilion of the Asikaga Shogun's palace in the fifteenth century. Of all applied arts, only Ikebana is truly Japanese.

The tea ceremony, "sado," is the most important of Japanese practical arts. Tea was used by Buddhist monks to stay awake during long sessions of meditation, and the ceremony itself was formalized in the fourteenth century. Tea is served in a sparsely-furnished room with only a single scroll painting and perhaps a flower arrangement in a precise pattern. The room reflects the ideal calm and tranquility of the universe.

Tokyo is also the national capital of performing arts, and both Japanese and western performances are featured at Tokyo's music halls and theatres. The most famous of the Japanese theatrical arts is Kabuki—characterized by brightly-colored costumes and music from drums and the lyrical samisen. The Kabuki-Za Theatre in Ginza is the major center of Kabuki in Tokyo. The National Theatre, near the Diet Building, also gives Kabuki performances.

Once considered vulgar by the wealthy Shoguns of the Edo period, Kabuki grew with the patronage of the newly-wealthy merchant class. By the end of the 1800's it had become both fashionable and legitimate. In early presentations, women were forbidden to appear on stage, and young men performed even the most erotic female roles. As Kabuki became more socially-acceptable the stories became less carnal though men continue to play female characters.

Music is an essential element, usually provided by hand drums, a flute, and the "samisen", sort of a Japanese guitar with three strings. The plays seem inharmonious to western eyes and ears, for though the plots usually revolve around some sort of personal emotion—guilt, social obligation, tragedy—the dialogue is incomprehensible. But the beauty of the costumes, the striking poses of the actors, and the alternately lyrical then harsh music attracts legions of western devotees of Kabuki.

Not only the music of the Kabuki theatre fills Tokyo halls, for the Japanese long ago developed a taste for the melodies of the West. The Tokyo Metropolitan Festival Hall features western performances including those of the Tokyo Philharmonic. Fabulous Suntory Hall, in Akasaka, stages both musical concerts and dance, including "Buto," the modern, expressive Japanese dance form. Buto has perhaps received more acclaim around the world than any other contemporary Japanese performing art. Not only is it more adaptable to the Japanese physique, but it expresses social concerns unique to the Japanese.

Dance, like other forms of art, is pervasive in areas of Japanese life not usually associated with the arts. When visitors see the three-hundred-pound sumo wrestlers on the streets of Asakusa or Ryoguku it is difficult to see them as artists, but in fact Sumo wrestling is called the "national skill" in Tokyo and is as respected as any of the fine arts. The rules of sumo are simple: The loser is the first wrestler to touch the mat with any part of his body other than the soles of his feet. The huge wrestlers, clad only sort of a white loincloth, may appear flabby but are in fact muscular and powerful. Their movements in the ring are guided by over two thousand years of tradition, and are as much choreography as sport.

Sports heroes are revered in Japan as elsewhere, but none receive more public acclaim than the giant Sumo champions. Their schedule is long and difficult, including both physical and philosophical training. Observers who watch work-outs in any of the stables that are open to visitors are quickly impressed by the work that goes into preparation for matches. The match itself, however, rarely lasts more than a minute, and may be over in fifteen seconds. Wrestlers, especially the national champions, are paid well and can afford to live luxurious lives when they are not in the ring.

The other event that dominates Tokyo sports pages is one that is truly foreign in origin: baseball. That the Americans have the nerve to call the victor of their World Series the "World's Champion" has always irritated Japan's rabid baseball fans. Indeed, many American players have made Japan their second home, playing here after their careers in the West have ended. The fences are much shorter in Tokyo's Korakuen Stadium, so an outfielder who may have been a so-so hitter for the Yankees is magically transformed to a Babe Ruth in Japan.

Baseball is, in fact, even more popular in Japan than it is in America. Even high school tournaments receive extensive television coverage. The Yomiuri Giants are Tokyo's favorites, and when the team is in town the stadium is packed. Teams are sponsored by Japanese corporations, and generally take the name of an animal: the Kinetsu (a railway) Buffaloes, for example.

One western corporation has captured the hearts of the Japanese without adapting itself to the eastern culture. Even Tokyo youngsters cannot help but love a mouse in short pants or a duck in a sailor outfit. Tokyo Disneyland is exactly the same in Japan as in America. Only the language is different.

Tokyo has a world of entertainment and culture—from Sumo giants to Mickey Mouse, from ancient porcelain to Pablo Picasso. What else would you expect in a nation that virtually worships art, in both her museums and her day-to-day life.

NHK Symphony Orchestra

Western music is played in ultra-modern and accoustically-perfect concert halls, like the NHK Hall in Shibuya. The Japanese have made important contributions to modern classical music, foremost of which is the famed suzuki method of instruction that has produced so many Japanese violin prodigies.

Suntory Hall, Akasaka

Among the most strikingly-modern concert halls in Tokyo is Suntory Hall, built by a liquor company of the same name. A huge pipe organ dominates the hall, in which all manner of western classical music, from opera to ballet, is performed.

Kabuki Theatre

During the Edo period, kabuki became the theatre for the masses, gaining respectability only after the return of the emperor to power in 1868. The earliest crowds were often drunk and rowdy. Gradually, the plays became more sophisticated and more accepted by upper levels of Japanese society and today kabuki is considered an "elevated" form of traditional entertainment.

Kabuki Theatre

Kabuki has remained unchanged for several centuries. Music, from traditional instruments, is an important part of each presentation. Women were barred from appearing on stage in early Japan, and to this day men continue to play the females roles.

Japan National Ballet, Sun Plaza Hall

Japan National Ballet, Sun Plaza Hall

Western ballet was not performed in Japan until recently, some think because of the scarcity of long-legged dancers. Post-war Japan has, however produced some of the world's finest ballerinas.

Tokyo National Museum

National Science Museum

National Museum of Western Art

Tokyo National Museum

Ueno Park is Tokyo's major cultural centers, with four important museums as well as a number of historic shrines. The Tokyo National University of Fine Art and Music is here as well.

Tokyo National Museum, Ueno Park

The Tokyo National Museum is the largest museum in Japan and houses the nation's greatest collection of Japanese art and archaeology. The centerpiece is the main building, where most of the Japanese collection resides. Other buildings contain art from the rest of the Far East.

Sumo wrestlers

Japan loves her sports heroes, and the sumo wrestlers who train in stables in Ryogoku and Asakusa are both worshipped and paid well. Though they appear to be overweight and lumbering, they are in fact muscular and move with surprising quickness in the ring.

Sumo wrestling

Sumo wrestling has been practiced in Japan for at least two thousand years, its skills having a grounding in Shinto religious beliefs. Most wrestlers are at least six feet tall and tip the scales at over 200 pounds, and wrestlers of twice that weight are not uncommon. These two in their black loincloths (color denotes level of skill, with white being better than black), are beginning a match that may be over in as little as fifteen seconds.

Tokyo Disneyland

The Japanese version of Disneyland is exactly like the original in California. Less than an hour from downtown Tokyo, Disneyland has taken the nation by storm and is one of the most popular tourist destinations for Japanese visitors to the capital.

Golf driving range, Shiba

Tokyo Racecourse

The Japanese are serious about sports, either as participants or spectators. Golf is among the most popular of amateur sports in Tokyo, and many hotels feature golf driving ranges on their roofs. This range, though at street level, accommodates over a hundred golfers at the same time.

Yokahama Baseball Stadium

Post-war Japan welcomed much that was decidedly American, baseball included. Today's Tokyo fans are every bit as dedicated to their game and to cheering on their favorite team as are those who frequent Yankee Stadium in the Bronx.

La Tour d'Argent, French cuisine in Tokyo

In addition to virtually thousands of Japanese restaurants, Tokyo offers visitors dining from every corner of the globe. La Tour d'Argent, one of Paris' most respected restaurants, has a branch in Tokyo, at The New Otani Hotel.

ACCOMMODATIONS

Hotels, Transportation, Dining

It's plain, from the very moment one sets foot on the tarmac at Narita Airport, that Tokyo is a city dedicated to the comfort of its visitors. None of the hassles to which travelers elsewhere have become accustomed—surly or nonexistent hotel staff, public transportation that seldom runs on schedule—haunts visitors here.

Security at Narita is thorough and reassuring and the only thing about travel in Japan that could be termed an inconvenience. The sixty kilometers from Narita to downtown Tokyo isn't the prettiest ride in Japan, but it is quick and comfortable. There are limousines that go from the airport to every major hotel and several train lines that serve Tokyo rail stations.

Everything runs on schedule in Tokyo. Trains are safe, fast, clean, and on time. The entire subway system is color-coded, and subway maps and signs are in both Japanese and English. The subway systems connect with JR (Japan Railway Companies) at numerous terminals, giving riders easy access to destinations outside the city.

There are three train lines operating in and around Tokyo. Both the Teito Rapid Transit Authority and the Tokyo Metropolitan Subway serve stops in the Tokyo metropolitan area. Japan Railway Companies is a nationwide rail system that includes the world-famous "Bullet" trains. Combined, the three lines make the world's most efficient public transportation system.

Subway etiquette takes a bit of getting used to for first-time guests in Tokyo. During rush hour subways can be crowded, and a normally-polite Tokyoite can be surprisingly aggressive when he has an eye on empty seat.

There are buses on Tokyo streets, but without basic knowledge of Japanese it is difficult to figure out the routes or the bus stops. For those who prefer to travel above street level, taxi cabs are a better bet. Drivers are courteous, helpful, and honest, though not all speak English. Some cabs are equipped with coin-operated massage cushions and color television.

Japanese hospitality continues upon reaching one's hotel. The selection ranges from the ultra-deluxe to small, Japanese-style lodging. Some hotels specialize in business visitors while others serve the tourist trade. In the upper priced hotel categories English is spoken by everyone, so those who find language difficulties awkward may want to stay away from the small hotels.

Tokyo is a sprawling city, so most visitors choose a hotel based on their interests. For culture and sightseeing, the Marunouchi-Imperial Palace hotels are good locations. Business travelers also look to Marunouchi, for it is close to Tokyo's corporate headquarters. For nightlife, look for accommodations in Shinjuku or Ginza. But no matter where one's hotel is, Tokyo's excellent subway station puts the whole city at the hotel's doorstep.

Like fine establishments in any international capital, Tokyo hotels feature swimming pools, health facilities, salons, boutiques, and restaurants. Little things separate Japanese hotels from those in London or New York, however. Service is flawless, despite the fact that there is absolutely no tipping, and guests are usually provided with cotton "yukata" robes.

Near Ginza, the Imperial Hotel is generally recognized as Tokyo's best. Its older tower dates from 1890, though on the inside the amenities are ultra-modern. The Palace Hotel, overlooking the Imperial Palace and gardens, is a popular business address, for it is close to both the commercial center of Marunouchi and Japan's political heart.

Another Tokyo hotel that is world-renown is the Hotel Okura. Near Roppongi, it is regarded as one of the best hotels in the world. The Akasaka Prince, in the neighborhood of the same name, was completed in 1983. An ultra-modern lobby of white marble sets the stage for its bright, efficiently-furnished rooms. The Prince hotel chain has modern establishments throughout Tokyo and other Japanese cities. Also in Akasaka, The New Otani, a sprawling multi-towered complex, is the largest hotel in the East. Its grounds feature a 400-year old Japanese garden.

At 45 stories, Keio Plaza Hotel, in Shinjuku, is Tokyo's tallest. Though its concrete-and-glass tower is formidable, its interiors are neatly-furnished and comfortable. Aoyama's President Hotel is generally thought of as the best medium-priced hotel in town.

The large international chains are well-represented in the Japanese capital. There's a new Hilton in Shinjuku not far from the Hyatt. The Holiday Inn is at the Tokyo City Air Terminal.

For those who prefer to get a little closer to traditional Japan (and who are not frustrated by an occasional language problem), a good choice may be a "ryokan," or Japanese inn. The rooms are furnished in "futon" cotton mattresses, and feature sliding paper screens and Japanese ornaments. Though generally more expensive than standard hotels, a ryokan often includes two authentic Japanese meals daily.

Tokyo dining can truly be a global experience, everything from French bistros, Italian ristorantes, and delicatessens crowd the streets. Virtually every country in the world is represented. The Japanese love to dine out, and estimates of restaurants in Tokyo range as high as fifty thousand.

They range from the "ryotei," expensive traditional restaurants, often with geisha service, to the inexpensive noodle restaurants. Usually an introduction is required for a foreigner to visit one of the former. The average restaurant is small, often a family-owned business in which the mother acts as both cook and hostess.

Guests in Tokyo always remember the plastic models of food in restaurant windows, and have been known to drag waiters to the sidewalk to indicate their choices. Japanese food is increasingly popular in the West, but there is a lot more to the national cuisine than sushi and tempura. There is a 2000-year old tradition represented in Japanese restaurants. The basic Japanese meal consists of rice, soup, and fish with pickles and vegetables served as side dishes. Meat has appeared on Japanese plates for only the past century.

Hospitality is cordially offered by all of Tokyo's hotels, restaurants, and shops. It is hard to imagine that it has been little over a hundred years since Japan was opened to western guests, for it seems in Tokyo that there must be centuries of hospitality behind the modern welcome extended to everyone.

The New Otani, Akasaka

Akasaka Prince Hotel, Akasaka

The New Otani, Akasaka

Century Hyatt Hotel, Shinjuku

Akasaka Prince Hotel

Every major international hotel chain in the world is represented in Tokyo. The amenities they extend to their guests are definitely world-class: boutiques, shops and salons, swimming and fitness facilities, fine dining, even golf driving ranges. Service in every Japanese hotel is impeccable, a feature of every Tokyo business in the hospitality trades.

Tokyo Hilton International hotel, Shinjuku

Keio Plaza Hotel, Shinjuku

Multi-story restaurant, Shibuya

Noodle restaurant, Aoyama

Ginza coffeehouse

Plastic food in a Shinjuku restaurant window

Japanese restaurants run the gamut from tiny noodle houses to the ultra-deluxe. Some of the finest casual dining is in the small restaurants in older neighborhoods like Ueno and Asakusa. The ultimate in Japanese traditional restaurants are the ryokei establishments, geisha restaurants frequented by Tokyo's top executives.

Italian restaurant, Ginza

Tokyo restaurants span centuries as well as cultures. The city boasts hundreds of dining places that serve the newest in ethnic cuisines, often in the city's most dynamic new buildings.

Buses in Shibuya

Japan Railways

The "Bullet" Train leaves Ueno Station

The Ginza Line, Tokyo Station

Public transportation in Tokyo is the world's most efficient. Trains run on time, are always immaculate, and stations are safe. The subway system is easy for the first-time visitor to understand, and can put the entire city at one's disposal.

Taxi cabs in Ginza

日本石油

BUSINESS OVERVIEW

That Japan has become a powerful economic force in the modern world is an understatement. The country is the major trading partner of the United States and is considered the world's leader in many industries. Our one-time enemy in Asia is now our strongest ally there.

Around the globe Japan is synonymous with names like Panasonic, Mitsubishi, Sony, Toyota, and a dozen others. One of the nation's most phenomenal accomplishments has been to turn the tide of opinion regarding its products. At one time, "Made in Japan" meant cheap, poorly-made, worthless. Today, American consumer publications routinely list Japanese automobiles among the best-engineered and most reliable vehicles in the world. Professional photographers have foresworn their favorite German cameras in favor of those with names like Nikon, Pentax, and Canon, all made in Japan.

It has been scarcely forty years since her manufacturing sector was virtually destroyed by Allied bombs. Japan works with limited natural resources, having to import virtually all the nation's energy, steel, and a host of other basic products. Yet not only has Japan been able to grow from the ashes of World War II, her executives have learned how to do business with buyers from all cultures, from every corner of the globe. How has the island nation accomplished so much in the fast-paced world of international trade?

The answer: Cooperation. Every sector of Japanese society is determined to meet economic goals realistically set by those who participate in commerce. The government, like others, publishes both long and short term plans for development. The difference is that the plans are the work of not only bureaucrats, but also represent the thinking of business leaders and academia. Therefore, the mercantile community never feels like government goals are forced upon them.

This group management extends to every level of Japanese business. The Japanese management style has often been called "management by committee" or "management by consensus," for many decisions are made by groups of workers, technicians, and executives. Business pronouncements thus seem to come from the bottom up, rather than from the top down. Employees at the lowest level have a feeling of having participated in decisions that guide the future of their employers.

Decisions are not simply handed down, they are hammered out at what seems to westerners like endless conferences and meetings. The process takes a long time, but when a decision is made everyone in the organization—from the rank and file to the top management—knows the why and how of the project as well as their particular role in it. Once a decision is made it will be implemented quickly and efficiently.

Of course, the existence of this management style is directly related to centuries of Japanese socio-cultural development. Group harmony is the major guideline to Japanese behavior, and groups of importance include not only one's family and social circle, but increasingly, one's employer. The Japanese corporation has become a quasi-family, a small village set in the midst of Tokyo. Dedication to a company is demanded of all employees. Accepting a position in a major Japanese company is more than just a job. It is a commitment to a lifetime of adherence to company goals and rules. The corporation is an interwoven community in which all employees share a common destiny.

Employees arrive at their careers following intense examinations at both high school and college levels. Companies often select a large proportion of their staffs from favored universities. Their recruits have an emotional loyalty which surpasses any employer-employee relationship in the rest of the world. Firms provide housing, transportation, medical care, and even vacation villas. In return for the intense loyalty, an employee is virtually guaranteed a secure job for the rest of his or her working life.

Japan's international trade is virtually controlled by five thousand trading companies, called "shosha." A trading company is a marketing organization that operates on many levels. It may own both wholesalers and retailers, shipping firms, and banks. This makes international markets accessible to the thousands of small and medium-sized Japanese companies that make up 98% of the nation's economy. A trading company like Mitsubishi acts as a major manufacturer, distributor, banker, and developer.

Only ten of the thousands of trading companies handle half the nation's trade, companies like Mitsui or Mitsubishi. But it is the small company which is the backbone of the economy, for small firms provide a chain of subcontractors to fill the manufacturing needs of the Nissans and the Sonys.

Increasingly it is more than the products of Japan with uniquely Japanese names emblazoned upon them which have come to represent the Japanese economy abroad. Tokyo has quietly become the financial center of the world's fastest-rising economic region: the Pacific Basin. The Tokyo Stock Exchange is now the largest trading floor in the world, measured by the number of shares that trade hands daily. The world's largest brokerage firm calls Tokyo home. Japanese stock traders are making a mark in the West as well. Their influence in New York has been referred to as the "sun rising over Wall Street," a reference to the Japanese flag, a single red, solar-like sphere on a ground of white. Japanese investors pump over $100 billion into American stocks and bonds annually.

Japan is moving towards a service and financially based economy, partly out of self defense. Other Oriental nations have emulated their success, and as a result are beginning to beat the Japanese at their own game. Korea is producing automobiles that have been well-received in the West and other countries have begun manufacturing electronic goods that sell below Japanese prices in American stores. It is natural to expect Japanese businesses to adapt to the changing economic scene around them, adjusting their product mix to the competitive environment in which they find themselves.

It is the individual that forms the backbone of both small and large firms. Without the dedication, the long hours, and the sacrifices that Japanese workers are willing to give to their company and their nation it would be impossible for Japanese goods make their way to every corner of the earth.

Tokyo Stock Exchange

Tokyo Stock Exchange

The most up-to-date communications equipment is used on the floor of the Tokyo Stock Exchange. Stocks and bonds of both Japanese and international companies are traded in what at times seems like a tumultuous exchange. A guiding rule of this, the largest stock exchange in the world is, however, that "all trading on the exchange be conducted fairly and smoothly." A computerized trading system as well as an automated market information system digests and reports data, providing moment-by-moment information to investors and brokers.

Sumitomo Bank, International Trading Desk

Sumitomo Bank, Ltd.
Along with 223 domestic branches, the international network of Sumitomo Bank covers thirty countries, making it the fourth largest bank in the world. Founded in 1895, Sumitomo has grown to be Japan's most well-capitalized and most profitable bank. Sumitomo has aggressively pursued both commercial banking and industrial development financing, and is one of the leaders in Japan's efforts to diversify her economy, lessening her dependence on manufacturing and strengthening her financial sector.

Nippon Telegraph and Telephone Corporation

Nippon Telegraph and Telephone Corporation

NTT has for decades been a leader in Japanese telecommunications, and is now leading the industry into a new era following industry deregulation in 1986. The corporation, in addition to serving the day-to-day communications needs of a growing economy, maintains nine research and development laboratories that investigate potential new services, integration of world-wide unications, and improving service to her millions of customers.

"Media World," at Sony headquarters

Sony Corporation

In 1986, Sony celebrated its fortieth anniversary, four decades which have made the corporate name a household name around the world. The earliest successful product was an electrically-heated cushion, and since those early days Sony has become the international leader in electronics development. The story of Sony is one of consistently high-quality merchandise and astute marketing.

Ricoh, Atsugi plant

Ricoh

The Ricoh plant at Atsugi is the centerpiece of Ricoh's manufacturing operations. Office automation products, notably laser copiers, are developed and manufactured here.

Nippon Kogaku (Nikon), Sendi plant

Nikon, Sendi Plant

Ricoh, Atsumi plant

Shiseido Company, Ltd., Beauty Research Lab

Nikon (Nippon Kogaku K.K.)
Nikon is well-known for its high quality cameras and other photographic products, but the firm also manufactures precision instruments and ophthalmic products, and engages in bio-medical engineering. Since its establishment in 1917, Nikon has set the world standard for optical technology.

Shiseido Co., Ltd.
Shiseido grew from its base as a pharmaceutical manufacturer in 1872 to one of the world's leaders in the cosmetics industry. With broad commitments to research and development, Shiseido uses the latest bio-technical equipment and techniques to develop safe and effective cosmetics.

Japan Steel Works, Ltd., Yokohama

Japan Railway Company, Ueno Station

Japan Air Lines

K. Mikimoto and Company, Ltd., Toba Pearl Works

The Japan Steel Works, Ltd.
The Japan Steel Works was established in 1907 as a joint venture between a Hokaido shipbuilding firm and two British corporations. It is now an integrated manufacturer of steels and machinery with a world-wide reputation for quality.

Japan Airlines Co., Ltd.
Japan Air Lines has a worldwide system of nearly 200 thousand route miles, serving sixty cities in thirty-four countries. The company has pioneered much that is accepted as routine in modern air travel: executive service to business travelers, frequent-flyer programs. Service board JAL planes is gracious and hospitable, in the best Japanese tradition.

Japan Railway Companies
Japan Railway Company began in 1907 with limited service between Tokyo and Yokahama. Today, the firm maintains over 21 thousand kilometers of track and serves the Japanese public through over five thousand stations throughout Japan.

K. Mikimoto & Co., Ltd.
In 1888, Kokichi Mikimoto established the first Japanese pearl farm, at a time when the culturing of pearls was little more than a theory. Nearly twenty years passed before the first marketable cultured pearl was harvested, but today Mikimoto Pearls are recognized the world over.

The Port of Tokyo

The Port of Tokyo

Tokyo has been one of Japan's leading ports of call since the Edo period. Today, there are the most up-to-date port facilities to serve the world's largest container ships.

Izu Peninsula
The hot spring at Izu was founded in the eighth century and is one of the oldest in Japan. The drive along the mountainous Izu Skyline Parkway boasts dozens of spectacular views.

SURROUNDING AREAS

As much as Tokyo represents all that is modern in Japan, the surrounding countryside embodies the traditional spirit of Japan, definitely a more relaxed environment. The urge to flee the city strikes both tourists and natives, and the hot springs and mountain ranges just beyond the Tokyo suburbs attract millions of vacationers each year.

There was a time when the distant peak of Fuji-San, Mount Fuji, was visible from downtown Tokyo. But with the ever-present smog of the growing capital, such days when Fuji makes her presence known are rare. Fortunately, it is but a two-and-half hour ride from Tokyo by bus. To climb Fuji once is, according to Japanese lore, a sign of one's wisdom; to do it twice is to display one's foolhardiness.

Yet over 300 thousand people make the six-hour trek each year (it only takes four hours to come down, and there are plenty of rest stops and snack bars along the way). The volcano last erupted in 1707, and now shows signs of being nearly extinct. It has long been a symbol of the Japanese gods, and until the Meiji Restoration it was forbidden for a woman to climb the conical peak.

At the mountain's southern base is a mirror-like lake that often bears the reflection of Fuji on it glassy surface. The Japanese know it as Ashinoko (Reed Lake), but foreigners call it Lake Hakone, after the town on its southeastern shore. To the north and east of Fuji-San are the Fuji Five Lakes, a major resort area. All the lakes are surrounded by villas owned by corporations and universities, and provided to employees and students as sort of a benefit. The largest of the five lakes, and also the highest, is Lake Yamanaka. There is excellent trout fishing, boating, hiking, and camping. The villages are dotted with shrines and small temples.

From Odawara south on the Izu Peninsula, nearly every village is a hot spring resort. The peninsula begins at Atami, Japan's largest such resort and a town that has been unceremoniously dubbed the "Las Vegas of Japan." Atami is blessed with hot springs because of its location at the edge of a volcanic crater. The public baths here are not to be missed. While those attached to the hotels, reserved for private guests, are all utilitarian ceramic tile and chrome, the public baths sport palm trees, ornate rock formations, goldfish, and a view of the surrounding terrain.

A bit further south leads one to Toba, on the Shima peninsula. Ise Shima National Park, which occupies a large portion of the seacoast here, is renown for both its natural beauty and its Shinto shrines. But it is pearls that bring most visitors here, for on Pearl Island, in the Toba Harbor, Mikimoto Kokochi produced the first cultured pearl in the 1890's. Today, Mikimoto pearls line the shelves of the world's most exclusive jewelry shops. A model pearl farm and pearl museum is open at the Toba plant.

The Tokyo-Nagoya Expressway continues to the southwest toward Japan's early capital, Kyoto, a day trip from Tokyo. Kyoto was founded over a thousand years ago, and was the imperial capital until 1868. Kyoto has over 200 Shinto shrines and 1500 Buddhist temples and would take a lifetime to see completely. Heian Shrine is tops on most visitors' lists, a reproduction of the first temple built in 794. A short walk takes one to the Silver Pavilion, a manor built in 1482 by the Shogun Ashikaga Yoshimasa. Niji Castle was built by the first Tokugawa Shogun and is an example of the very best of ancient Japanese architecture.

Every shrine, pavilion, or historic site has its own garden. West of the Nijo Castle is one designed by one of Japan's most skilled architects in the seventeenth century. The garden that surrounds the Katsura Imperial Villa, considered by many to be the most perfect of gardens, was designed by a Japanese landscape architect 450 years ago.

While Kyoto is the early imperial capital, Nikko, north of Tokyo, is the Japan warlords, of sword-bearing generalissimos, and of ancestor worship. It is the center of the Japanese Shinto religion, a village of shrines, pagodas, and temples. The centerpiece is Toshogu Shrine, a gilt and lacquer monument nestled in the woods. Thousands of towering cedar trees line walkways between the religious monuments. Gates are carved with mythical dragons, clouds, and flowers.

A character from the novel "Shogun" is immortalized here, Tokugawa Ieyasu, who was the model for the book's Japanese lead. The famous Shogun is buried in the mausoleum in Toshogu Shrine, and for the 350 years since, buildings have been kept in pristine condition. The pagoda, temple buildings, tombs, gates, even the storehouses, drip with carving and gold gilt. Nikko is a mountainous resort area of extraordinary beauty and for that reason is a perfect setting for the nature-worshipping Shintos.

Nikko is along the eastern foothills of the Japanese Alps, which offer good skiing in the winter and hot springs in the summer. The Siberian winds blow the snow to the mountain ranges along the northern edge of the Alps. Ikaho, on the slopes of Mount Haruna, is one of Japan's most popular resorts. When skiers are not on the slopes, the wildflowers of the flat plateaus attract thousands of hikers.

It is amazing how rapidly the years roll back on almost any road out of Tokyo. To the inexperienced, Tokyo seems unpardonably modern, especially in contrast with the slower, more traditional countryside. Yet it is this countryside that is the roots of the great capital city, and most of the capital's residents are but one generation removed from the villages and fields on which Tokyo seems to encroach.

The Japanese Alps

The Japanese Alps
Japan's Alps, just two hours from Tokyo, provide recreational opportunities in every season. The mountain range has some of Japan's top ski resorts, and the natural beauty attracts hikers throughout the warm seasons.

Lake Yamanaka

The Fuji Five Lakes

At the base of Mount Fuji are five lakes, to the north and west of the famous mountain. Japanese and foreign visitors alike stream here in the summer for boating, fishing, camping, and hiking.

Atsumi Peninsula

Atsumi Peninsula

The Atsumi Peninsula is opposite the Ise Shima National Park, and is one of Japan's natural shoreline wonders. Japan, though scarcely larger than California, has more coastline than the entire United States, much because of its ruggedness and its many breathtaking coves and inlets.

Odawara Castle

Odawara Castle
Odawara, with its historic castle and several museums, is the gateway to the Izu Peninsula. Trains run frequently from Tokyo's Shinjuku Station to Odawara, and from there visitors can explore the peninsula's natural beauty and historic sites.

Toshogu Shrine, Nikko

Tokugawa Ieyasu, Nikko statue

Toshogu Shrine, Nikko

Tokugawa Ieyasu was the first of the Tokugawa Shoguns, and was responsible for joining the warring city-states into Japan's first semblance of a national government. Nikko is his artistic masterpiece, much based on Chinese influence and decorated with gold gilt and vermillion. The shrine and burial place of the great shogun is the focal point of Nikko.

Nikko Sunset

Kyoto

Nijo Castle, Kyoto

Nijo Castle, Kyoto

Nijo Castle is perhaps the nation's best example of Japanese architecture and landscaping. Built by the Tokugawa Shogun in 1608, the castle was a home to Japanese regal leaders until 1939, when it was given as a gift by the emperor to the people of Kyoto and opened to the public.

Father and Son at Sensoji Temple